The Tall Golden Minute

THE TALL GOLDEN MINUTE

LINDA SAUNDERS

TREMAEN PRESS

This collection copyright © Linda Saunders 2023

All rights reserved

The right of Linda Saunders to be identified as the author of this work has been asserted in accordance with Section 77 of the UK Copyright, Designs and Patents Act 1988.

No part of this book may be circulated or stored (or otherwise retained) or lent, resold or hired out in any other format without the explicit written consent of the Publisher.

A CIP catalogue record for this book is available from the British Library

ISBN 978-1-7397814-9-1

Tremaen Press is the poetry imprint of
186 Publishing Limited
Published by 186 Publishing Limited 2023
www.186publishing.co.uk

Acknowledgements

Thanks are due to the following publications in which some of these poems have appeared:

Acumen, Artemis, Broken Spine, ffraid, Magma, Origin Stories: An Anthology of Beginnings, Raceme, Poetry Salzburg Review, Poetry Wales, Scintilla, Tears in the Fence, The North, The Tree Line: Poems for Trees, Woods and People, Ware Poets Competition Anthology, Wells Festival Competition Anthologies

'Tresure' won first prize in the Second Light poetry competition 2018

'Lifer' won third prize in the Wells Festival International poetry competition 2018

'Outside Chance' won first prize in the Teignmouth Festival open poetry competition 2019

'Handyman' was commended in the Acumen poetry competition 2020

'Everlasting Flower' was shortlisted for the Bridport Prize 2020

'Our Brocken Spectres' was commended in the Second Light poetry competition 2020

'Everlasting Flower' was commended in the Ware Poets open poetry competition 2022

'Two Wood Pigeons' was highly commended in the Wells Festival International Poetry competition 2022 and won the People's Prize

I am hugely grateful to John Freeman, my editor at Tremaen Press, for believing in my work and for his invaluable suggestions and critical insight. I am ever grateful for the friendship and mutual support of poets with whom I have shared poems and whose feedback and comments have been helpful and encouraging over the years, particularly S.J. Litherland, Frances-Anne King and Lesley Saunders.

Linda Saunders

As a one-time fine-arts journalist, Linda Saunders found an early spur to poetry in a wish for a less analytic language in which to speak about art. As Philip Gross has written, 'she applies words to subtle experiences as a painter might use paint'. A keen bird watcher, she is fascinated by fleeting visual events, as well as by feelings glimpsed 'sideways', 'between the visible and invisible', as one poem has it. For her, 'writing is a way of exploring and listening to both the external and the inner world, to others and myself. The sounds and resonances of words are vital to me, and a means of discovering elusive feelings and experiences.'

Her poems have have been published in many magazines such as *Agenda, Acumen, Poetry Review, Poetry Ireland, Poetry Wales, The North, The Rialto, The Warwick Review*, and a number of anthologies, including *New Women Poets* (Bloodaxe) and *The Tree Line* (Worple Press).

Her first full-length collection was short-listed for the Jerwood Aldeburgh Prize, and commended for 'gently passionate poems whose luminous apprehension of the natural world and of subtle human gestures is tempered by a fine poetic wit, a sharp eye and a keen ear.' She was also shortlisted for the BP Arts Journalist of the Year Award.

Previous poetry collections by Linda Saunders
She River, Vane Women Press, 1999
Ways of Returning, Arrowhead Press, 2004
The Watchers, Arrowhead Press, 2009
A Touch on the Remote, Worple Press, 2016

*for Barney and Eddy
and for my granddaughter Bethany*

Contents

Now in the Dale

His Distance	3
Orange Poppy	5
Now in the Dale	6
Slipstream	10
Second Nature	11
Swifts Are Nesting	12
From the Bridge	14
The Tall Golden Minute	16
Drought	17
Lifer	18
Spirit Guide	20
Sentinel	22
Love Poem to an Ornithologist	23
Voices	24
Possession	25
The Grass Becoming	26
Shadow's Shade	27
I Am Beck	28
Swale Time	30
Our Brocken Spectres	33

Under the Birch Tree

Ancient Spring	37
Sudden Spring	38
Hortus Conclusus	40
Two Wood Pigeons	42
Internal Window	44
Up	46
Tall	47
Strength	48

Handyman	50
(Through Headphones)	51
Visitor	52
Counterpoint	54
Of Blades and Seeds	56
Bliss	58
Silversmith Raising a Vase	59
A Moment's Flight	60
Everlasting Flower	61
LIVE SLOW	62
Wild Mushrooms	63
Living Statue	64
Defiance	65
A Touch of the Air	66
Such Presence	67

She'll Come Out Running

The Skeleton Houses	71
Almost	72
Perch	73
She'll Come Out Running	74
French Lessons with English Tea	76
Outside Chance	78
My Mother Being Very Deaf	80
Under the Hat	82
Towards the Horizon	84
The Tree	85
Conjunction	86
First Word	87
As*ton*ishing	88
Aperture	89
Fleet Feet	90
Making Him at Home	92
Joy Ride	94
Too Soon to Winter	95

Gift	97
Lift-off	98
Before I Can Fly	99
The Blue Mountain	100
Snow Shadows	101
Tresure	102
Beyond Me	103
Moss	104
Night Vision	105
Notes	107

Now in the Dale

His Distance

He seems both grand and vulnerable
in my window seat, so I settle for one
that's unreserved across the table.
Already he's opened a laptop, plugged in
his phone like any seasoned traveller,

though he looks weathered by wilder journeys
than this by train heading up to Glasgow.
I could see him leading a camel train;
in a jostling souk rolling out his rugs;
on a fishing smack, bucking the high seas.

He's wearing a black wool hat, cone-shaped
like a gnome's, counter-balancing a black beard
streaked with silver below cheeks scored by who knows
what pilgrim trials. He pulls the hat down now
over bushy eyebrows and his eyes. He sleeps.

He sleeps through Warrington and Crewe, crackly
intercom announcements, thudding doors
at further stations north, and on through
Preston, Lancaster, Oxenholme, while England
streams by, green and rumpled, sun-flash on cars,

may in the hedgerows, hazy shrug of fells,
as gradually I've become aware, beneath
the train's rumble and sway, of another rhythm,
a quiet tide's shuffle in and out across shingle,
the regular susurrus of his distance –

which lingers, an aural after image,
long after I've arrived, and in the garden

later, as I tune in slowly to the birds,
summer migrants staking their claims, whittling
the spacious air with song: between and behind

the willow warbler's cascading notes, so
sweet they're almost sad, surely it's the wind
breathing softly in the trees' fresh silks
as I wonder if he's still asleep, sleeps
all the way to the terminus, and beyond.

An Orange Poppy

for Leslie Santos

To quit expectancy, as the wise counsel,
is to make room for luck, random, choosy
as a windblown spark. As this stroke of flame –
these flighty silks right at the door, beside
the slab of stone where I painted the Cott's name
twenty years ago, among veined pebbles,
rocks winking with mica, trophies from walks
that have collected round a few leggy herbs,
creeping mosses. We tried a rose here once,
but it failed at the wall's north face, though blue
cranesbill flourish in the ground beyond.
Everywhere, wild yellow poppies spatter
the darkest days and cracks with proxy sunlight,
their black-pepper seeds flouting the parable
in ramshackle walls, any drill of dirt.
But time and again I've failed to host
their orange sport, poaching pods that whisper
ripeness from shy clumps around the village;
I still find seams in coat pockets gritty
with forgotten hopes. Yet this gift alights
out of nowhere, bright petals uncrumpling
almost too subtle to the touch to feel,
pollen-gilt anthers springing from their heart
as if astonished, too, at a trace of gold
on my thumb. Only now, this shrug of grace –
such brazen modesty! – a strike of joy.

Now in the Dale

Change barely
              perceptible
till the sun prises open
a rack of cloud:
seeding grasses receive fuzzy haloes,
each tall-stemmed buttercup
              a lick of fire.

        So still –

        the beck has forgotten
its moil and tumble
after last month's deluge,
lolls now in umber pools
joined between rocks by
              fine silver screws.

        So quiet –

except for that chaffinch
chip-chipping among hazels,
their branches above the stream
supple, buoyant, just stirred by

        a passing grace –

        easy, easy

the spread leaves seem to gesture
with a balancing motion that would play
down, quell, all fear of change.

*

Three trout
          just so long,
fry becoming fish,
frill-tailed, dorsal-finned, balancing
          the beck's flow,
enough of it after small rain
and clarity in the shallows
for the slippery light to invent
substance from shadow,
to freckle and play them now
along the stony bed:
follow my leader, the longest,
the other two quick in her wake,
weaving upstream a few yards
          then whipping about
to shoot a slim rapid between two rocks.
Like nine-day lambs, like dogs in snow, possessed
of this novelty, this what-to-do-with
          life, this water.

*

Now it's the ox-eye daisies
          yearning
from the bank on raggy stems,
all one way reaching all agog
sunny side up for the sun, dizzy
stunned Catherine wheels
wide-open white around
honey-plush hubs, whirligigs
of love-me love-me-not love-me
          O love me...

*

Rumour of storm,
                        sycamore leaves wagging,
so-so, they are all warning:
a wind's front agitates
                        the edges of things.
Leaf-hands flickering
break patches of sky into nervous cut-outs,
an illusion of dazzle
                        against lowering cloud.
Not a ruffle in the dregs of the beck
though maybe it feels,
as I do now on bare arms,
the first infinitesimal prickles of rain on its skin.

*

The moment when
                        everything takes to the air
this let-up, this lull
between rain thrashing the trees, whelming the lane
and the next scowl of the storm –

                        a chance for flight
                                      rise
of winged things too quick and transparent to see
into the brief time of their lives
                        on a wind
now almost gentle, come-hither

as sunlight cases the damage:
                        tall grasses
(yesterday nose-high) every which way
tousled, only thistles and hogweed
unbowed on the verge.
And swallows speed-feed

over field and churchyard, shimmy-skim, swoop,
white rumps of martins
                               flecks of flying light
in this fairground of air.

*

On a low thermal
                  fluff-borne seeds
from the willow herb's jubilant spires

                  float

over walls and fields on parachutes of light
to glide and turn
                  in a slow pavane
on no breeze to notice
while the hirondelles wheel
in the middle distance

                  between here

and Green Bell – itself so still,
yet the fell's long tide

                  that sweep and curve

joins at its own remove
the dance of seeds and birds.

Slipstream

I noticed stalactites under the bridge
today for the first time, after twenty years
inspecting air, sky and the state of the beck
with a mug of tea fifty yards from our door.
Suddenly seen – as if they could be sudden
after how many score of their own years, drip-
fed by pale salts leached from the stone arch –
just finger-length, like sugar cigarettes
we used to suck to sticky points as children.

Lengthening invisibly as our lives shorten,
they reach as if for its speed towards that sleek
current careening across limestone slabs, clear
as amber ale in the glasses of drinkers outside
the King's Head, who lean on the wall
as they set the world to rights, just glancing
sometimes at the bright stream, but unlikely
to remark those tapering fingers, or a fish
idling below the dark span of the bridge.

Second Nature

Truth, said Trout, is the stream and my body
telling it. Absolute and nothing but
the glovely fit of me and medium,
constancy, the cut of fin to current.
I know exactly what I need to know
to hang in here between the shantung light
and rippling shadows, all eye and gills and
supple scales. Truth is my elastic spine,
my balance. There is no room for error,
thought, between my nature and the water.

Truth, said Man, lying under the willows,
is ticklish, slippery, and so beautiful.
Slides a bared arm slowly into the dark
water, downstream of his quarry, waiting
as his blood cools, clever hand and fingers
learning the river's wiles, becoming weed
wavering on the current, never still:
so lyrical is guddling, love and craft
exquisitely laced together, desire
refined by intent – so intimate and other.

Swifts Are Nesting –

in the house over the road that was not there
   when we first came, in the plot of shaggy grass
      that was an orchard before our time, above

the meeting of waters, Steps Beck with Scandale,
   before they wind through Smardale to the Lune –
      in the new house made of stone from tumbled barns

and sheer defiance that relentless winter when
   the diesel in our car froze, and the landlord
      of the King's Head pronounced across the bar

as if casting a curse, there'll be ice in the mortar,
   it'll never set, so we half expected those walls
      rising in our view to rumble down one night,

but he was wrong; Alan built the place for himself
   with the craft he'd forged over years in hand
      and heart, but sold it on when times got rough –

in the house that faces the morning sun, which finds
   after rain the colours of mussel shells, moonstones
      in the slates of the roof, so the teacher of maths

and his wife the doctor parked red and silver cars
   in the drive, and settled to stay, planting delphiniums
      with no knowledge of gardening, he said,

but they soared all the same to belfries of lazuli
   splendour by the door they painted willow green
      into the house where Katie was first thought of,

who shoots up too now, a daughter with eyes to mirror
    the bluemost gaze of our Himalayan poppy,
        which first flowered the very week she was born –

in the house where they've been fretting
    this June about mice in the loft, all that squeaking
        and scratching, till we call them to watch the swifts

flickering black and silver in the sunlight
    above roof and trees, harvesting sky, first one then
        another dipping down to nests under the eaves,

to deliver their beak-loads with only the briefest
    stalling of flight to their ravenous young. Just listen.
        Voices of ghosts speeded up almost beyond hearing.

Within weeks, scarcely fledged, they must follow
    the flock back to Africa, crossing mountains, horizons,
        seasons, deserts; but next summer the same birds

will return to this new-found home under an arc
    of trees: an honour, a gift, Katie's parents agree,
        a blessing on the house that was once not there.

From the Bridge

A few gold and copper leaves
on the stream's dark bed gleam
like wishes through the water's
amber deceiving
                strata;

a single yellow heart, just fallen,
rides the beck's dreamy slide.
Those that have sunk and settled
seem, to my unfocusing eyes,
                        to float

in uncertain space, between deep
time and the minute-hand drift
of that one small voyaging craft.
It fascinates, that tease
                of distance –

like those ovoids of spun fire
on our tv screens which conjure
objects whose remote blaze
has taken thirteen billion years
                      to find us,

anything older, farther
having not yet arrived, and never
may, since it's all expanding.
I'm pondering today's
                breaking news:

astronomers reach to the limits
of the observable universe
for three trillion galaxies, ten times

more than they'd thought –
                          vertiginous

just the idea of it, as I fathom
far clouds above canopies
of trees in the shallows below.
While the beck seems barely
                          to flow

under the yellow leaf, yet
the mirror surface shimmers,
quick with a swarm of vibrancies,
a quivering hatch
                    of light.

The Tall Golden Minute

I reckon they've finally given up
on the church clock and let it stand
for all time at midnight or noon;
despaired of oil and ratchets and cogs,
of web and bat and the cracked bell,
but painted the face instead, bright
gold for each Roman numeral,
defiant of all hours lost and to come.

Both hands together as if in prayer,
the tall golden minute hiding the hour,
point eternally up beyond the weather vane
whose arrow's fixed in flight to the east,
faithful to the prevailing wind;
point an aspiration higher by far
than the squat tower's castellation, than
rook and raincloud and shrouded fell.

Who'd swear anyway that time exists,
but only the exchange of then and now
between noon and midnight, this late sun
throwing shadows of trees not yet in leaf
across the glebe, so that celandines
purse their stars in the shivering grass,
though the clock face catches brilliance
still above the rising tide of dusk.

Drought

The last trickle in the beck
has stopped.
In remaining pools
where algae bloom in green clouds
on any rocks still submerged,
only the fry are moving,
inchlings needling around
as if wondering where to go, where to grow to.
A surface tremor
like a distant memory of spate,
or faintest hope,
troubles the deep reflections
of motionless trees.

Lifer

We used to think it a mad sparrow before
we learned it was the last migrant to return
and its name explained what it was up to,

flipping off a post or a low-slung branch
with flight controls seemingly gone haywire.
Today, here's the first, hunched at the ready

on the tallest tombstone in the graveyard.
Overhead, against a washed sky brushed
by feathery remnants of raincloud,

swifts are scything the wind, returned only
last week for their circus of high-flown love.
For our souls' health, we need to go on gazing,

stopped in our tracks and sorrows, to mark
the arrivals of birds that cross the world above
our news and wars, our migrations of loss.

Long-haul passerines with their songs of summer.
The swifts twenty-four/seven on the wing.
Birders call their first-ever sighting of a species

new to them, a lifer. For me, each returning
migrant is a lifer again, somehow newer still
in renewing each first of every summer

down the years: harbingers of memory,
human and avian, surely ancestral.
Yet only this moment recalled as exquisitely –

wing-tilt and flecked feather, the lilt of its whistle.
My heart always somersaults as crazily as
the spotted fly-catcher plying his skill under

the churchyard yews like a spirit liberated
from the earth below, skittish with surprise
and quite loopy with life, this fling of resurrection.

Spirit Guide

Between twilight and dusk –
pale shape of bird

lifts
over shadowed fields

wide-winged in a drifting glide
to climb – still low –

and cross our road
into the tousled slope beyond.

Even as we gasp
barn owl,

braking the car, dousing the lights,
it's gone –

oh but then swings
back in a steep arc

to float
over our way ahead

as if to lead us homewards.
And we follow

though we're homeless now,
lost, in thrall,

marvelling at a gift of wings
(snow-softly)

to power flight,
seeming scarcely to beat

but deeply stroke
the advancing night.

Spook-white, and still hungry
it veers again

and folds itself into the hillside.

Sentinel

Just a flit of shadow vanishing
into that sycamore. But ever-watchful,
searcher of skies, seeker of signs, you follow

and find it, naming the Little Owl,
bringing it into visible being
for a moment in our day: Look! Just there

to the left of that fork – while I peer
and scan, and see finally what might be
an upright fruit or cone, a wedge-capped

shield shape balanced on its point, oh yes,
a bird, framed in a sentry box of branches.
It bobs just once, like good day, or beware,

I've got you, too – with those great eyes
(in one so small) which funnel right into mine
through the binoculars I bring into focus:

a gaze fierce as fate, below a beetling frown
of ghost-white brows. It swivels its head
to case the field and hillside beyond,

and we keep very still, quiet, mesmerised,
longing to meet again those eyes that guard
the unknown at a frontier between worlds,

as if, gaze meeting gaze, we might step across.

Love Poem to an Ornithologist

How come a tailwind makes no difference to the record speed
a great snipe on migration keeps up across thousands of miles?

He draws diagrams, arrows to show the lift from below, pull
from above, of air responding to the beat of wings; the curve

of an aerofoil – the key, he says, to understanding flight –
within the spread shape of a wing. He talks aerodynamics

and thrust, as though the bird, I would guess, makes its own wind to
    stream
across the tilt and lilt of primaries. To launch a plane at sea,

remember, it must face the wind. But your bird would save energy
with a tailwind, he goes on, though the speed remains constant.

So it's a mystery – like your poem. A love letter, I say,
which will need the great snipe's super-efficient wings to reach you.

But I'm right here, he says. Though sometimes he's very far away.

Voices

The beck's back in business
                     busy-bodying
banks, bedrocks, weed,
guttural, gurgling, bickering with itself
in polysyllabic babel.
                   It's all crepitation,
Steve (a scientist) said once,
just the bursting of bubbles,
billions of them. Juggle
of water and air, incessant windy applause.

Listen
      to this
           subversive rumour
under the bridge – Steve,
articulate still if vanished and silent,
           here even now
among voices of the beck
which rummages on to the meeting of waters
                               downstream.

Possession

It's knowing what to look for. Where
and the fleeting when.
Getting your eye in
for a silvery flicker when the sun comes out.

Wings the size of my fingernail,
a sailboat sail when folded, freckled with light.
Then opening on darkness
beady-bordered with scarlet.

You'd never spot it but for the blink –
dark/light dark/light flash-fast here-and-there
low over grass, leafage, rock roses –
of flight:

        Northern Brown Argus.

To know it for myself. Not the sight only,
but to hold in mind like breath
the quick air, all the fragrance and keep
of the day's gift:

        beyond storm and loss.

As a child, I longed through a shop window
for a ship in a bottle, sails bellied
by mystery, doubly dispossessed
by glass.

Enough and more now to wait for the sun.
To follow a flicker
and wait for it to settle:
there.

The Grass Becoming

Today I'm in love with a kind of grass,
foxtails, preparing to flower from these heads
more like tails, erect on polished stems.

I stroke one upwards with its soft grain
of seed casings, exquisitely lapped, tight
as yet, and sleek. It slips through the groove

between two fingers and my thumb, firm
but silky, tapering to a tip that seems
to have a shy, almost animal urgency.

To describe bamboo, according to Hokusai,
one has first to become bamboo, though not
with words but his own sensitive brush

flexible as the leaf-blades of his subject,
a tool scarcely separate from his questing
hand and arm and eye, his breath and heart.

With what words of astonished art could I
become foxtail grass at this aspiring
moment before a wispy frizz of whiskers

will turn each tail into a seeding headdress
dusty with pollen? In love is my only
way of becoming the grass becoming.

Shadow's Shade

River Crowdundle, darkling and flashy
through the oaks' twisting limbs and
finger-flutter of ash: water-light

skims off the leaves' late-summer
sheen across tall wings of shade.
Deep among roots, between here

and somewhere, Ross buried Shadow,
while leaves seemed to hover overhead
quivering on windless currents.

He scrounged cobbles from the stream
to drop in the hole and keep from scavenge
that bundle of love, bone, old tartan rug

and shaggy fur brindled like leaf-litter,
before he infilled it with loam and rolled
a boulder across for guardian/gravestone.

He is shade himself now in the woods
he husbanded, while the dog, wood-wise
and nosy in their ever-after-life, slips

through water-light, leaf-light, questing.

I Am Beck

Mistake me not
           for brook
some Alice-jump
                  between lush shires
no simpering streamlet me
no purling rill in a cushy bed

quicker   wilder
              beck I be
                     becoming
river any moment –
                trickle to torrent
in a hectic dash from
                  my fell parent
who makes the storm with his frown
and passes it on
            to his offspring

Secretive   truculent
                 rocks in my throat
eels in my gut
           I can flash-flood   spate
drown a sheep
           wreak havoc –

following lullaby weeks of dazzle and dawdle
below milky ways of water-crowfoot
shade of alder and the lean-low hazel

with play-pools for trout
                    shelves and narrows
where they idle
            or lurk
                    in a slick of shadow
practice polish and vanish
in the camouflage speckle I taught them –

beck at my best
            idyll reflecting
                        dragonfly flicker
swallow-skim   daydreams   poised beak of heron

Swale Time

after reading The Order of Time *by Carlo Rovelli*

It could be there –
          where the view opens
into the dale beyond. I see us get out
of the car, the wind kind for once, sunlight gleams
on those eyetooth stones painted black to show
where, in snow, the road is. You could pitch off
the edge here when the cloud's down, blind fate
at the bend's surprise, or in level rain at night,
or dazzled, climbing west into the low sun.

We drive on east to Tan Hill, where bikers,
bandy and armoured, stand about with pints
at the highest pub in England. We don't stop,
so it can't be there, but follow the thin road
across the moor, hairpinning sometimes – Think Bike! –
into the groove of a beck, and out and on and then
coasting down as heather and sedge give way
to sheep-cropped verge above the wooded line
of the Arkle, to Reeth.
                    A thought search here,
in a crack of the cobbles or a divot of grass
on the green. A kind of listening, not believing
anything's lost ever, searching memory, too,
for the jingling Morris men we found there once
dancing to an age-old tune and knocking sticks.
It's when we leave that I first miss my watch,
hoping I left it at home, knowing I didn't.
So it happens, swinging up dale through Healaugh,
Low Row, Gunnerside, that we talk about time –

quantum, never and always, reality
not what it seems. I'm trying to understand

how the watch I may have lost in the valley
would lag a split jiffy behind the same watch
left high on the fell, each in its own moment
of 'proper' time on its unique world line.
The physics is a matter of gravity.
At some point of the day, my watch just slipped
into mystery, hidden in spacetime,
insouciant. Shock-proof, waterproof, always
constant, it must still be going, that treasured
gift, with its long history of friendship, lost
in shadow or rubble, or found by a stranger:
watch-bearer, time-traveller, I imagine her
gazing at the ocean's wake, or adjusting
minutes and hour as a plane cruises high
above cumulonimbus into another zone.

There we are, following the Swale upstream
to park at Ivelet Bridge, which humps a lane
across the river's liquid agate, gold-squiggled
over mirrored beeches and alders, deceptive
deeps. Then meadows in buttercup-blaze, fiery
plumes of sorrel, red embers of clover,
frail smoke of Queens Anne's lace. Black blink of
a chimney-sweeper moth. 'Hot enough for you?'
asks a portly man, trudging the other way.
My brown arm has a pale band where the watch
is not. Time-free now, I finger its trace.
Sandpipers flicker and pipe, as they do, probe
between stones for insect morsels, or pick them
from the water's lap against a rocky perch.
A fisherman stumbles through the shallows,
whipping his fly line across supple currents
to a deeper pool. Zag of electric blue.
                              Time
slows down as speed increases – think bike,

think rocket; at the speed of light it stands still.
As I do, lost myself in moment to blue
moment of speedwell, tormentil's lowly sunbursts,
with no way but hunger to mind how the day
flies on. A black rabbit freezes for seconds,
ears up, a keyhole of darkness on the path ahead,
an omen of death, some think, but it feels lucky,
and hard to believe it's vanished so fast.

Our Brocken Spectres

Surfacing from some deep abstraction,
he puts down *The Order of Time*, equations
swimming like plankton in the reach of his eyes.

He tells himself, and me, and the heat-struck
afternoon, that there's no such thing as Now,
trying to explain: his now can never

be the same as mine, though we sit as close
as this under the little Malus tree
whose openwork of branches affords

our sole protection from the sun. Indeed,
my ration of shade will creep over him
soon, and I must move my chair again.

A dizzy vision: Now is no longer
a universal main buoying us all,
but smithereens in a local, quantum rain:

my moment, his, yours and everyone's
being invisibly small, and theirs alone.
And I remember when we climbed through cloud

up to Red Pike and looked down, the strong sun
on our backs, each at a tall and spectral
self, thrown on a white quilt which obscured

the valley and lake below. I could see
only my own. He could not see mine.
Not shadows then. Each waved, arms like wings,

to singular selves, which signalled back, alone.
Together, apart, we stood on the mountain,
we sit in the garden, each and both

adrift in strangeness that feels like freedom,
and grief. Leaf shadows flit across my arm
as I reach out from my now to touch him in his.

Under the Birch Tree

Ancient Spring

after Victor Pasmore, *Song of Life*

The artist in old age made drawings
of an old tree, its crabbed branches wandering
across the paper's landscape, their outstretched
span supported by forked crutches
which lean and stagger under the load.

In some – as I remember – there is a bird
perched on a high twig or in flight
through space. Just an outline. In others
a mist of green, spring's emanation.
And his pencil made a spatter of small leaves

like floating raindrops
                        or notes of the bird's song.

Sudden Spring

We walked the other way round the park today,
which with the sun, so long absent till now,
seemed to sharpen our senses and surprise us
with new slants of the light, tilts to the paths,
the view at each turn rearranged, and then
as if circling widdershins had conjured them –
an eruption of little mauve crocuses,
hugging the steep slope in their hundreds
under the great bare limbs of the beech trees.
On a further grassy flank the yellow kind
were *manifold*, we decided, choosing the word
to express our wonder. We'd never seen
so many just here, taking over now
and ready to open a hosannah
of petals to the first full spring sunlight.

Squatting among the flowers a little girl,
about three, was not picking them as we'd feared,
but hunched low over them, nose down close.
Do crocuses smell? When she stood up straight
in her small boots, short legs in orange tights,
we held our breaths as she stepped so very
carefully between each cluster, balanced
by spread arms, not crushing a single crocus.
Was it her mother, watching from the path,
who had taught her child such reverence?

As we walked on, George turned to me
with that dawn look which lights his face sometimes.
My heart is singing, he said. He grew up
in the East End of London, in mean streets
smelling of hunger, bomb-snaggled terraces

in which a gap had once been called home.
He remembers, as he has told me often,
his first sight of something green, glossy leaves
of a laurel bush on a roundabout.
It was love, singing even then of escape,
a world of earth and plants and animals,
the woods he'd wander, watching, listening,
the miles and miles he'd traipse through wild country,
deeply lost at times, the mountains he'd climb,
finding his way down by starlight, singing.

Hortus Conclusus

Beyond the walls
and their wide moat of quiet,
thousands are dying.

Yet these days might be holy days,
a month of Sundays,
as we keep vigil under immaculate skies.

We've observed, close-to,
the particulars of spring's arousal:
along every twig and bough

of the Japanese cherry, buds
dark as scabs turned into pearls,
which split and spilled

a flush of diaphanous light.
Bemused by the swift
drift of days, their unseen terrible

freight, we can only review
a time-framed drama of growth:
one near invisible

sliver of green, at the tip of
a flailing twig on the birch
which today flickers thousands

on thousands of leaves in a breeze
that brings no tidings of contagion,
carries no sirens or bells.

Immured in beauty and fear,
we can no more hear the traffic
of souls than the fall of petals.

Only the blackbird whets his song
on silence, while hover flies hypnotise
the uncertain air between here

and grief's appalling distance.

Two Wood Pigeons

The lilac extends a woody limb,
crabbed with age yet springy, to offer

a welcome to this familiar couple,
plump and comfy on their rocker

as it dips and sways in the breeze
and under their meticulous preening,

enough room between them to stretch
a wing skyward, spread coverts and

primaries for inspection. Then each
pearl-grey feather lapped softly over

shoulders and back must be checked
and smoothed. Now the under-wing fluff –

fuss and draw that too through the beak's skill.
To take a peek and a peck below your tail,

coil your blue-grey neck over and into
a feather knot of the whole body.

Undo it, zip up long flight feathers again.
Lift a claw to scratch a putative chin.

Is a pigeon's work never done?
How can I describe it as thoroughly

as they groom, though I match their
diligence with my own watching,

forgetful of everything beyond
the process and precision of fettling

words that against all odds might lift, bear
and float their burden on air?

Internal Window

We pass things between us, memories that rise
like a genie from an old lamp rubbed clean,
from these jugs and teapots and bowls reached

down from a wide ledge dusted less than seldom.
We have washed and dried every one
to reawaken the gleam of the glaze

and the colours it protects undimmed.
He passes them back to me, where I stand
on a chair to replace them on the shelf

at the internal window that lets light through
from the hall to the kitchen. One by one,
he makes almost a rite of it, says Careful!

as if I would not be with these bygones
which we lit on once with glee and brought home
wrapped in newspaper. He can't help foreseeing

disaster – how china would smash if dropped
from this height. Though just an infant in the War,
he still hears the scream of sirens in his dreams,

the whine of doodlebugs over London, feels
through the years the aftershock of the bomb
that reduced their terrace home to rubble.

But now I too can't bear to watch the news.
Already millions of refugees jam
the routes out of Ukraine, trundling cases –

what to take? what to leave? – lugging plastic bags
stuffed with iron rations, nappies, a warm rug,
infants on their hips, wide-eyed, taking things in.

I receive each find, found again, in both hands
like a gift, as we tell each other where
and just when this lidless ginger jar, or this

teapot with its violets in fresh spring bloom,
first took our fancy, asking to be loved.
Familiars, survivors, viewed from each side

of the internal window they look somehow
astonished by the light of this moment,
rescued again from their own lost stories,

and part of ours, re-enchanted, at home.

Up

He jumps, legs straight for vertical take-off,
which happens for a moment, a few inches
before both feet jolt down on the path again.
He's four maybe, and eager to grow, stretching
his arms up in a V, hands now almost
level with his mother's head scarfed in black.

The grownups mooch around his sister's pushchair,
where she sleeps. The Chinese goose, lost and lonely
these years past on this reach of the river, skrawks
in the water below the railing, lifts wings
in sympathy with flight, but folds them back.

He spreads his fingers, swivels hands out sideways,
feathered serifs to his V, flaps them, jumps again.
Lands again, but gazes up to watch himself,
a boy rocket in slow motion, rise – higher
than the ginkgo trees' green crowns, that cruising gull,
St. Georges' flag flying above the Abbey.

Tall

A small girl is standing on the tall stump
of the silver lime, lifted there by her mother.

That famous tree had spread its shade across
lawns and arbours, towering to a record height

above Japanese cherries, magnolias,
squirrels begging from visitors paw on heart,

grandparents with push chairs, dogs on leads.
The stump is flat as a table, with curved

promontories once the low thews of the trunk,
a dark pitted centre the one sign of rot.

She is shaking bubbles from a kind of tube
filled with liquid soap. They detach themselves

from her wand, enormous, wobbling, floating
slowly away from her unaccustomed height.

Intent, solemn, she's possessed of a power
which shines in the brief lives of her progeny.

Above us, space is blue and cloudless, leafless,
deep with the tree's ghost, sorrow and wonder.

Strength

All night the great engine of the wind
did battle with trees in their full panoply
of summer leaves, not the flimsy silks of May
or autumn's brittle pensioners, but diehards
in their prime, tenacious, tough. This morning
the world's half buried in them, drifted in gutters,
cluttering flower beds, blocking paths and gates,
cars swagged in green. Behind our neighbours' house
a sycamore dangles two huge limbs, held
in precarious place by the canopy
and the last splintered hinges of fracture.

I've a grandstand view from this upstairs window
of three men who know what they're doing
with a grapple, ropes, a winch, and a harness
for the one high up there with a chainsaw,
his helmet shining like a giant red berry
in the ruffled foliage. They make it look,
not easy, but a matter of muscle,
of youth and daring, buckled to nous and skill,
men in command of this work and their bodies.

And oh, there's Roy, well into his nineties,
taking in the damage to his garden
from the vantage of three shallow steps
at his back door. He was treelike himself
not long ago, six foot four, and still might be
if he could unlatch somehow his folded spine.
With both hands moving in sideways shuffles
down the wooden handrail, his slow progress
is as gripping, almost, and as tense to watch
as the tree surgeon's wrestling with branches
in the height, amputated boughs crashing
through the rest to thud on to the lawn.

Roy's found a rake to lean on, and to work with
to the best of the last of his strength.
Any wind at all might blow him over.

Handyman

Keith the joiner
    everything-sorter
        knight in shining

    comes down his ladder in the wind

his new-moon-on-its-back grin   to explain
    what was wrong with that door
        a mean bugger

needing as it did   as we knew   that shrug
    of a just-so jerk   persuasion
        of elbow and wrist

and how he fixed it
    twiddling and twiddling
        his grapple of fingers

    the spark of his ear stud kindled by the wind

which snatches words as hands mime
    some tricky   diagnostics of locks
        and how he cinched   the gap

pinch of space between two fingers
    and a thumb   along top edge and lintel
        between left side and jamb

    he zippers the wind

rehangs the door on air
    swings it open – be my guest – so
        smoothly   closes it snug in its frame

    holds up both palms   forbidding the wind

(Through Headphones)

Alone in a room somewhere else,
he recorded his poems, woke them again
from the silence they shaped when his pen
scored the white of a page with their story.

Now, unembodied, he reads them aloud,
not out there in her room, but in the hall
of her head, nearer than close. She attends
to each inflection of voice, hearing him

trace words to their source in the intrigue
of detail with memory, the fetch
and feel of particular chances
that led to a poem, his tone wondering

and keen to realise a remembered music.
Some thrill of suspense she feels listening
to how he chooses, as he reads, where
to give weight, pause, relish, surprise,

reenacting the original choices,
almost, she feels, as if he is writing
the poem again, trying it on his tongue
for truth. She hears some nuance unheard

in her silent reading: how curious
he finds the world and his place in it,
each clue to the mystery compacted
in the ordinary matter of life,

a meaning within yet beyond the sense,
unnamed, unseen, except as a hat, a nail,
a quizzical bird, a wild rose opening
(now, in her room), nothing more than this.

Visitor

A sliver of light
            flitting
above the lawn, weaving,
wavering, never quite deciding

to settle, feinting as if to baffle
a predator, or searching the air
for some sweet pheromone –

a Holly Blue!
            If I look away
it must vanish, but now flirts
a flake of sky around me,

dancing a net to hold me captive,
then alights on my hand –
a pale blue sail.

Colour alive, silvered azure
with a sheen of turquoise,
never to be believed till now

as I dare bring it even
                closer
to examine banded antennae,
a pepper of black dots on folded wings.

Smaller than my fingertip,
sipping salt from my skin,
it investigates my strangeness

with no apparent notion
beyond its own need and moment
of the gift it entrusts to the human.

Intimate and rare,
                    remote
as a signal from a star,
I feel the tickle of its footsteps.

Counterpoint

A sound half-heard, too uncertain
to ask definition, but consigned or dismissed
to a frequency that knows its own business
without intruding on yours –

a sub-song, an ice-cream chime
muted by distance, or strain of cell-phone jingle,
drifted up from the city's basso profundo,
a ripple or riff of some forgotten theme –

who's listening anyway?
They've come here to look, gaze out
and down from this high proscenium
between beeches whose massive limbs lean

over them laden with summer leaves and mast.
The city of stone, pale and intricate
in its drench of light, seems leached of life
at this remove but for the flash of traffic,

the insect creep of shoppers along
the main drag, viewed with curious pity
from this superior air. Yet it fascinates,
the human: custom and commerce, their own

everydays, storied streets, landmarks, spires.
Arrived at this crest they pause, point,
lark about, take selfies against the view,
though someone has tied flowers

to the railings, and spilt a gritty dust
over the edge and a steep tangle of brambles.
But the music – is it? – comes from somewhere
else, or round the corner, where only a few

idle above a patchwork of allotments
before the hillside plunges again
into a lush vale. He is perched on a log
on the grass below me, busy with his hands

at something I can't see from behind,
except for a glint of silver, until
I hear again the liquid notes of a flute,
surely, that snatch or rumour of a tune.

A moment's quiet, like the green vale's breath,
and he tries again, the same phrase failing
at perfection, but aspiring. A call,
a message, a song healing an unheard

question, reminding of birds, flutter
of breeze in overhanging leaves, a shoal
of bright fish threading the hearts's reef –
woven of mourning, yearning, and delight.

Of Blades and Seeds

Today I will walk across the arena,
as I call it, a broad green space away
from the popular viewpoint, a clearing
favoured by solitaries, where the beeches
extend their own graceful serenity
over the slow dance of a figure
absorbed in Tai Chi perhaps, mindful movements
swimming on air, or sometimes there's a girl
meditating, sitting in Zazen and a force field
of stillness.
            I pick my way across roots
down the tricky slope where I slipped once and fell.
I am careful, determined on my course
though a man is practising Karate –
a splayed angular crouch, then a zig
a zag and a high kick, freeze again,
now hands slicing the air to define
and defend his space, to warn off and keep
a stranger at bay. At each chop and thrust
I catch a quick sigh of the air or release
of his breath, but I stick to my path.

He pauses, straightens, and Hello, I risk
like a password – which dispels all threat.
What a beautiful day, we agree,
and that May is the loveliest of months,
the beeches' new leaves as supple as silk
and through-lit by the sun with brilliance
on the fan of branches above our heads.

His black T-shirt sports a bold design
in neon orange – a pair of orchids.
His students have made a special study,

he tells me, and the school is renowned
for that work, collecting seed from round the world,
sending it to Cambodia to restore
beauty to a landscape ravaged by war.

Then he talks of Japanese Karate,
which develops strength and balance, each move,
or kata, has a name and a meaning.
He lifts his arms – raised hands, tall fingers –
to look up and through the gap between them
at leaves which shift softly to filter blue sky.
This is called Kanku Dai, look at the stars.
He relaxes and holds out his palms to me.
Do you know the meaning of Karate?
Empty hands. So he faces friend or enemy
without a weapon, gives or defends
with those hands that can chop and swipe like blades.
I see the hands of children offering seeds.

It's time to leave him to his practice.
When I walk away his spirit will tauten,
poised at the ready for his warlike dance,
a peacemaker, lover of orchids, leaves,
stars, on the arena under the trees' grace.

Bliss

The birch tree stands like a great bird
airing many wings. Each pendant heart-
shaped leaf tapers to a point, hundreds
to every supple twiggy cascade.
Rain falls gently in the still morning
to favour one then another with a single
drop. Every leaf, a tongue lolled and
longing to taste the blessing with a dip
of pleasure at each hit, funnels love
along the groove of its spine to the tip,
quivers then resettles among the rest.
After a month of drought, the whole tree
is blessed, seems to twitch, thrill, tick
all over as each lucky leaf takes its catch –
with what might be a note struck by skilled
and subtle fingers on the celeste,
if only I could transcribe such music.

Silversmith Raising a Vase

To raise: to make to rise
   from a sheet of metal perfectly flat
a vessel, vase, or ringing shell

   to cause, originate and bring about
through an act of will, of art tempered by skill
   it happens through relentless wounding

to bring up a question or a child
   these cruel inflections in unbroken shine
he chooses the first hammer

   to instigate, incite and animate
pock pock of hooves round a well of shadow
   the sound more like a pang

pang-pang pang-pang each mark each mark
   a heart-beat letting in the dark
to hoist and elevate a flaring rim of petals

   to rouse, from sleep or death
the form's idea, his not-yet-born, to beget
   and bring into existence, foster, rear

such argent beauty

A Moment's Flight

It's a day for watching cricket, indoors,
on screen. He's riveted to a scene where
the rain's holding off and the fielding side
is all in green-man green, vivid defenders
of a storied realm: a long view holds them,
formal, ready, as the bowler walks back
for his run, and I look in to say goodbye.

The air is my mood's double, glumly chill
with a heavy drizzle, as I trundle
a trolley along the tarmac aisle past
bumpers of parked cars, an empty vista
which I scan quickly before crossing.
A girl, I think, though it's hard to tell
at a distance, in silhouette, arms flinging

up to lift a running leap, legs arcing
wide then clicking heels mid-air – I never
see her land, just that moment's flight across
the gap. And she's gone, leaving an after-
image of pure exuberance, bequeathing
its levity to this masked world, and
something like joy hovering in my mind.

I'm back, I say, passing through with a quick
glance at the screen, in time to see the slow-
motion replay of a catch. The green man,
straight as a young tree, needs no flying stretch,
no acrobatics, as the ball descends
from on high like destiny, near vertical,
towards his hands, which open like a flower.

Everlasting Flower

The young man on the bus has a blue rose
on the back of his hand, a life-sized bloom
in its prime, elaborately, exquisitely etched
into skin and shaded to show the curl
of petals unfurling from the hidden heart.
Lean as a blade, he is pale in his black
bomber jacket and black-rimmed specs,
as if like his ghost-blue flower
he too had grown indoors in the dark.
The young woman beside him is soft
for his sharp, noonday to his dusk,
not beautiful, but 'bonny', in a word
from another time which becomes her,
wholesome, warm as the beech-brown
of her coat and that glossy fall of hair.
An unlikely pair, yet familiar, you can tell,
and quietly safe in their ease of belonging.
He fidgets with his phone; she's as composed
as a field of ripe grain on a still day.
On leaving the bus, he hands her down:
perhaps she is carrying a secret,
which he knows already, and guards.
Before they're lost to my sight, a wind
lifts her hair like farewell. I imagine
how long the rose will last: how it may
float like a dream still over the mottles
and corded veins of an old man's hand?

LIVE SLOW

He overtook me, elbows working,
sneakers kicking back the pavement,
and the two words on his T-shirt
that looked painted in white brushstrokes
right across stooped shoulders –
stooped, his pace suggested, by the head's
eagerness, an intensity of gaze –
the long breath of those two words
gave permission
                for the world to pause,
look about, breathe, reflect,
though I wanted to rush after him
to say, I love your T-shirt and those wise
white words on soft sage green
and the loose swing of cotton
from shoulders that have borne weight
(really he was quite old) and philosophy.

Could be his slow-living requires
acceleration to expand the moment.
A dancing insect fits its whole life into just one
of our flash-by, disregarded days,
and the camera's thousand blinks
slow into visibility those beating wings.
So the quick eye, thought-flicker, may catch
a truer vision.
                Way ahead now,
that man, neck and neck
with the livelong instant of his passing day.

Wild Mushrooms

I roll back the hems
from their dusky gills,
white pithy domes;

strip off limp flags
tenderly, deft
as a nurse with bandages.

I am the cook, a healer.

I've seen mushrooms bubble
through tarmac,
splitting the black crust

like happiness.
My hands smell of caves,
sweet mortality.

I peel mushrooms
as if to peel mushrooms
were to live slowly.

Living Statue

Two white geese ride the river's polish,
and now a figure dressed in light –
what little there is – pushes a bike
along the towpath: scarcely a knight
in shining armour to rescue
a forlorn afternoon, yet silver
below the gold-leafed tulip trees.

He tethers his steed to the railing,
glances toward my seat, and nods,
almost in collusion, wry or weary,
as if we've found each other out
in life's green room, off-stage.
The eyes look sore, red-rimmed
in his precious skin, gleaming paint
or make-up discovering every crease
and wrinkle of a surface chased
with secret hardship and humour.
Silver fingers place a cigarette
between silver lips, inwardly
the colour of a wound. The brief
flame lends brilliance to his chin.
Smoke floats quickly to nothing
above him; skeins of foam weave
and unfurl on the water's current.

When I see him next, frosted and
frozen among the high-street crowds,
I'll drop gold in his cap as tribute
to his art, my pledge of belief
in wonder, and he'll make his slow-
motion knightly flourish of thanks
to a stranger, who might be a poet
cloaked as usual in shadow.

Defiance

Tulip trees along the river walk
hold on to brown and brittle flowers
like bundles of faggots, once those strange
chalices licked by fire and hidden
in summer behind the leaves' massed shields –
all down now, and pasted to wet tarmac
in a collage of rusting yellows, drab
ghosts, beside puddles pocked by raindrops,
ripple-ringed:
                there's much I can find
to love, these lingering late days, most
of all the trees' defiance, seeming
to brandish their extinguished beacons,
to remind or promise, or be touched
alight by this young woman, a walking
rainbow in a rose-pink coat, which parts
at each brisk swing of indigo tights
to reveal a flare of turquoise skirt.

She flouts November's grey, which has doused
the leaves' late blaze of yellow and clouds
my mood, though I keep panning for gold
from the swollen river's weave of colour,
olives, duns, below a lace of foam
unravelling, and two ducks riding
the race, beaks at stretch as if they would
catch, pass, at the river's pace, that bright
girl striding away into her summer.

A Touch of the Air

I stand up in the cafe to pull on my cagoule,
fumbling for armholes, but the hood unscrambles
of itself, lifts, drops, and settles lightly
across my shoulders, as if haunted.
Some uncanny attendant, just a touch of the air,
preempting a need with such easy grace.
A voice from on high behind me whispers,
not to frighten perhaps, Perfect, so I turn
and glance up into a face broad and lofty
as the moon, grinning down on my surprise.
I feel like a child, or old, a small creature
to be helped by one more powerful and skilled.
No time to find words or be astonished
before he goes out into the rain unthanked,
unprotested, unsolved as a being
who knocked softly at the door, then vanished.

Such Presence

At a distance, from the path above the house,
the silver birch appears to lean. Another storm
is forecast: Eunice, sweetly named, could have gusts
of hurricane force. But the tree's winged height
is braced, I must believe, by its counter-image
below ground in the intricate strength of roots.

I can't bear to watch for long from a window
as the storm punches again and again
like a battering ram, and the whole trunk rocks
and judders from base to branch-tip, twigs in flight.
We wait it out. The tree withstands the assault –
this time. My body aches with the struggle.

I don't want to outlive her, exposed to clouds
and the naked sight of neighbourhood houses,
to a space unfilled, unsheltered, ungraced
by countless flickering leaves. The lifespan
of a birch tree is between sixty and ninety years,
though some may see well over a hundred, more.
Forty years ago, she already towered above me.

Now she is grand, queenly, robed in summer.

Zones and passages of her youthful pallor,
gullies smooth to my fingertips, pattern her trunk
between the bark of maturity, dark, craggy
as a landscape of dried lava, cruel to the softness
of my palms when I press against it to take
strange comfort. It's a kind of intimacy.

Trails of snail slime glint in the sunlight like veins

of her own ore, winding up and up, further
than I can trace them into her complex heights.
Why do snails climb trees? There are theories –
to escape beetles? – but I touch the mystery,
resistant as this bark to my skin; upwards
is enough as the meaning of life for now.

Most mornings early, I go outside to greet her,
mad enough to use words, say hello, and watch
for an answer, an exchange of signals, blessing
in the swing of leaves, a flurry or a single
flutter, on the stillest day the merest breath
as if feeling for my own.
                              There will be winds,

fatal storms – as there will be wars – then more storms
we give our human names to, as if to own them.
I don't want to outlive her. Such absence.
Standing under the birch tree gazing up,
lost in the interplay of leaves and sky,
I can't tell joy from grief, or grief from joy.

She'll Come Out Running

The Skeleton Houses

Weekends, when the site was quiet, mixers idle,
we claimed freehold of rubble-strewn rooms,
scratching our spells with knuckles of chalk
so they'd spook through plaster to freak out
the future home-owners and give us invisible
passage through their Chubb-locked lives.
Rick peed in the hearths to discourage their fires;
I risked the stairs to creep across their nightmares
as they tossed on memory foam in the master bedroom.
We howled and hooted in their undreamed Beforetime,
our cacophony stored with the builders' fag ends
and coke cans in the hollow-core of the walls,
to return as weird echoes behind their TV suppers.
We buried a mouse in a kitchen, with full honours.
Lenny walked the plank from scaffolding and fell
feet first like a cat, two storeys to the ground.
His small ghost dusts down his shorts to this day,
spits on his palms, limps off, says *Don't tell Mum.*

Almost

You could lose yourself even now
in the wood's bewilderment, stalked at dusk
   by that childhood story: the three of us
where the path divided, so one must split
   off from the others to test a theory that
the track meets itself again, quite soon,
   both ways curving sweetly like brackets
through ferns and dog's mercury, friendly arms
   around a tear-shaped spinney.
                                    You'll remember

how it felt then to be the forest's only child,
   tripping over roots in the twig-snapping silence,
mouth purple with juice, spooked by white
   destroying angels, cracking unripe nuts for pale
kernels of hope – the path fading into somewhere
   else.
         In the wood's silent theatre, listen

to the sub-song of birds, sap-song of oaks, sift
   of generations of summers. First leaf falling.
Find yourself now in the heart's clearing,
   this spell of no wind to speak of that has the year
on precarious hold, though leaves and the story
   are no more still than your own breath and blood:
sense them trembling in the moment's balance
   on an edge, the between of summer and winter,
yourself and the others, outset and homing.

Perch

I was taking photographs of my mother,
who kept protesting, of course, demurring,
though she was looking better than she had for years.
I'd lost the usual knowledge that she was dead,
and the gratitude that goes with it for a gift
of extra time. She did have some rendezvous,
a date to keep, which meant that we would need
to separate later. Always restless
anyway, she perched now on the arm of the seat
where I was fiddling with my camera.
I'd forgotten that perch of hers, nerved
as if for take-off at any moment
with a flick of resolve. *Turn round, Mummy,
I want you in this shot.* But she looked away
past a line of cottages, their plaster
and weathered beams mellow in the sunlight,
japonica flaming on the near wall,
perfectly photogenic. *No, this way,*
I objected, *I don't want your back view.*
She swivelled round, straightening a little,
preened almost, and I clicked the shutter twice,
while my own blink seemed to eclipse her face.
I thought I might ask her to look over
a letter I was drafting in French –
that would please her. And we could converse
in French sometimes, not to become rusty.
But no, it was hard enough in English
with her deafness. A cloud must have dimmed
the day's clarity. I wish I'd taken more
photographs of her, and could have kept them.

She'll Come Out Running

I saw my mother's beauty for the first time
when I was six or seven, and have kept it
like a small coin struck with her image,

still true, holding love's value, if smoothed
by the rub of memory across absence.
I'd never before looked to appraise or remark

a quality independent of a frock
patterned with hearts, diamonds, spades and clubs –
the one I loved, and later dressed up in – or

the amber necklace, warm at my own throat
on occasion now. I watched her dressing
sometimes, from my father's side of their bed;

she'd pirouette in her French knickers, flimsy
brief culottes, playing to her audience of one,
but I didn't think to label her lovely, just

my mother with the secret romance of years
before I was born, gaiety recaptured from
a lost world known as 'pre-war', which hung

about her in a whiff of eau de parfum.
I didn't think she was young. But one day,
coming home from somewhere with my father

in the car, we found her standing on the steps
to welcome us, caught in a rare moment of
stillness, she who was ever on the move,

in a dash, unlike my father with his gift
of calm: 'You watch, she'll come out running',
he said once, as we waited outside a shop.

But now at the door she surprised me
with something pure: the woman alone,
a self apart from all roles, purposes, to-dos,

revealed in her evanescent beauty.
I think I too felt distinct from that moment,
cut free to observe her across a lawn,

across years, finding myself groundless
as she was long ago, running, or in a flying
leap, badminton racket aloft, air

between the earth and her feet.

French Lessons with English Tea

for John Freeman

Learning how your father loved France,
and hearing him speak French in your poem,
I thought to tell you that my mother
was a Francophile, too. During her year
at the Sorbonne, when she must have been twenty,
she became engaged to a Frenchman, but
began to doubt, so she told me much later
as a kind of wisdom I should keep in mind,
whether she wanted to bear his children.

She took me to Paris when I was thirteen,
and a man pinched me as we strolled along
the Champs Elysées, a surprise that would not
translate into any language. She warned me
about the awful tea in little bags on strings,
but booked seats for a show, innocent herself,
she seemed to claim as the curtain rose
on a tableau of gorgeously plumed birds with –
Oh sorry, darling, I didn't realise – breasts.
The evening comes back as a lush scent
that wafted off the card in my programme
with which I fanned myself in the French gods.

The French onion seller was welcomed
at home with English tea, while my mother
drew him out with Gallic enthusiasm
and reminiscences. The handlebars
of his bike were relieved of at least two strings,
which would hang for months on the kitchen door.
He was not the only impromptu guest,
for my mother loved every foreign tongue,
even – sympathique to excess – catching

a trace of accented speech from a stranger
picked up (as my father teased) on the train
from town, like the 'Polish count' – But he really
was, darling. Terrible time in the War –
who stayed on for supper as well as tea.

Who might I have been, I often wondered,
if she could have imagined bearing
the Frenchman's children. Not me, certainly,
in fact no one at all, without my scatty
English father, who was thrown into a hedge
from his motorbike, taking a bend too fast
in his frantic resolve to call on her father
and ask for her hand. Scruffy on the doorstep,
dishevelled at best, surely he could never
deserve such a blue-eyed bilingual belle,
but who could resist his wild look of love?

Outside Chance

Baby wants new shoes, he'd say, to give a lift
to a small flutter each way on a horse
he'd wised up on in the racing columns.

But once he put all of five pounds to win –
and did – on an outsider, Burlington Arcade,
having dreamed himself among a wild crowd

yelling its name at the finishing line.
It was the sole evidence he could ever claim
for divine or psychic intervention

on behalf of any need of baby's
or his own. Just chance, he thought it, when a shell
slammed down beside him on the battlefield

and did not explode, while the world paused
as he said goodbye to it, aged seventeen –
he'd lied about his age to volunteer –

then found his glasses by another miracle,
and put them on to look into the future.
What is the difference between luck and grace?

His golfer's swing was an action of honed
grace, preceded by a moment of stillness
something like prayer, club raised on high,

as if to align himself with every
quick nuance of this world's here and there,
the sky's depth, each inflected shadow, tilt

of wind and wish towards a promised land.
Among his silver trophies on the sideboard,
sharing the pride with ebony elephants

paraded trunk to tail, were the egg cups
awarded in those days for a hole-in-one.
A stroke of grace, I'd say, in league with luck

that the shell didn't kill him, as was the perfect
loft and flight he gave a ball that landed
sweetly on the green and trickled home.

My Mother Being Very Deaf

I put my lips right to her ear
when she was dying
behind the curtains on the ward:
the send-off

she always needed at the door,
the seal of approval, affirmation
that the visit had gone well
and she could relax now,

being loved.
I felt she would hear me
in the dunes of her dying,
where she waited between each

and the next
last breath
for my kiss of a word
in her ear.

For years it was a problem between us,
the need to repeat, shout,
misunderstanding,
humour gone flat,

but one day, inspired,
seeing her tv listener,
its mic suckered to the box,
I plucked it free

and spoke into that.
A miracle!
We could chat quietly, laugh,
as I rediscovered

her forgotten mind,
as crisp and edgy as each magnified sound,
her impatience, too quick as ever
to finish my sentences.

Now I dabbed cologne on a hanky
and held it to her temples,
remembering that cool, astringent
comfort to my childhood fevers.

Whispered goodbye,
as I might blow on a remaining spark,
believing I reached that self,
still sharp
        as a star.

Under the Hat

My father didn't remember his mother,
all he had was a studio portrait,
black and white of course, taken for her wedding,
as you'd guess from that floral pyramid
of white marguerites above the flirt
of a brim – a fabulous hat, perched
above a cloudy fringe of dark curls.

Below such a phantasy, at that shy moment
in the camera's eye, how can one picture
reveal the woman, just a girl really
trying on a role with a hat, and speak to me
across more than a century's depth
with a secret smile to dispel the sadness
I read in her face like a premonition?

I search the pale oval for what it withholds,
the quick tease of bright eyes, words too soft
to catch at a distance. The mouth is soft too,
the full upper lip vulnerable,
expressing somehow such a sweetness
of nature, where I can see my father,
the injured innocent of the lost story
he carried with him, hers and his own.

Deep behind silence, could he have preserved
an aural trace of her stranger's music,
the foreign tongue she might have murmured
to this restless infant, her third, in her womb?
He never told me, maybe never knew
she was an Austrian Jew, inventing her
for me, and himself I think, as white Russian,
a Polish countess, which I believed enough
to boast at school of my exotic bloodline.

Years after his death, his older sister
revealed their mother's origins, hushed up
at the time, she said, though no one
appears to know how she came to marry
my grandfather – discovered, rescued
or rushed to his surgery with some illness
while travelling abroad, or did he meet her
wandering himself in what unnamed city?
Her story hides now in an oblivion
deeper than the photo's dark background.

Towards the Horizon

A small craft slips beyond the harbour wall.
At once a breeze takes the sail's red triangle.
Who knows where she's headed?

Sometimes I hold my father's watch on my palm,
the heavy bracelet hanging limp from my hand
while time slips like breath between my fingers.

He told me when he wrote from hospital
how he'd watch the second hand track round the dial
and how long a minute seemed that way.

Perhaps it stopped once, the minute and his life
on hold, till he shook it and felt his own pulse
restart for a while, though it would not be long.

The artist has caught the moment just before
the sail disappears into the sea's quietude,
a stroke of paint, a small flame never quite doused

in waves cast in rare metal in the setting light.
It can feel like that from here, a boat sailing
not into the future, but into the past.

The Tree

for Eddy i.m. Penny Saunders d. August 2022

Just to get it in the house must have been a feat
to match his courage in conjuring
the great family festival as always,
even this year –
                a mother of a tree!
Its tip nudges the ceiling as if to push on
through it. Bushy and bountiful, it over-fills
its corner, resplendent above trestle tables
imported as usual to seat this big family,
with friends and unforgotten single souls
who'll each get a present along with the feast.

Now the polished glasses catch rainbow fire
from fairy lights garlanded along branches
like wedding finery among birds and bells
and shining fruits, memories unwrapped and
reawakened as he cried – the children too,
all of them crying – each treasure dangled
or balanced by careful fingers to be admired
at a distance for the whole effect, such beauty,
the tears all part of it –
                a bride of a tree!
Now it's all hands to the kitchen, back and forth.
Ben, a paper-crowned magician, has followed
her famous recipe for home-made pudding.
Everything is ready, a cracker at each place.
Scent of resin pervades the room
                        like her absence.

Conjunction

So I dash out into the dark
and lean on the gate to train binoculars
above the hillside trees, and sure enough –

the moon, waxed almost full, sails
through wispy clouds which cross it in wavelets
like thoughts, brief shadows of emotion

passing. And Jupiter's tiny spangle
hangs above it, faithful as if tethered
by an unseen thread to the shining crown.

I could have missed it. Such beauty, I tell him,
texting my thanks, though mostly it was the cloud
that moved me with that sense of sorrow clearing

across a face (and my memory of his first word,
pointing at a switch on the wall, *light!*)
and the light in his voice, not yet of hope

or promise, but a beam of the old wonder,
at the dance of constellations, mystery
and order beyond his grief.

First Word

Not a command, or even a request
in expectation of action
from the Being who is so kind
but often slow to catch on.

This may be a different tactic,
a new sound, quiet and to the point
(for he *is* pointing – at the switch
on the wall, way out of reach
for someone whose very short legs
can still let him down with a bump).

But it's more, and has been dawning
not sure how long, deeply,
before daring this opening gambit
in a conversation that would share
a great discovery.
     Light,
he says.
   Indeed he's lit up with it,
has touched the invisible fuse
between cause and effect,
not just between switch and light –
which is marvellous enough –
but between word and world,
every
   thing
      in the beginning
alive in its name.

As*ton*ishing

for Barney

                     I loved the way he said it,
with that small explosion of the second syllable.
He was reading on a voice mail, from far away
in locked-down California, a poem he'd found
about an otter, and how a trail of bubbles
lifted from its dive through the water.

I don't want to find and read the poem, or not yet,
because he'd seen that once, he told me, the otter
swimming, and I've overlaid the poet's words
with his own account in a lit picture, played
for myself repeatedly, like a movie clip
backed by the timbre of his voice.

Memory shimmers the happenstance of event
and feeling, like the shift of light through water.
The poet had surely precisely evoked the scene,
but which then, it seemed, detached itself
from the words to leave an after image
in my mind, whose wake of silver bubbles
was something I can only call

joy. I asked him when he phoned today
what for him was the feeling of astonishment?
Perhaps he might describe a sudden thump
like a fist hitting his breastbone, followed
by a small rush of wonder along his veins –
that's what I felt, the way he stressed it.
He thought a while, but then said only
that it was always something about the light.

Aperture

His notes above the image on my screen
sent thousands of miles in a few seconds
tell me he saw it, this *golden-crowned kinglet*,
heard the song. *Low light*, he explains, *no flash*.

It gives softer pictures, but they're beautiful.
Late November branches present a tableau
of seasons, two rusty crinkled leaves, the last
of summer, with winged seeds hitching a future

from the wind, while every twig is arrow-tipped
with buds, quiescent, ready to shoot in spring.
And there's the bird, caught in its moment, still
flying undamaged through a cage of time,

grey wings fanned wide, blurred faintly with speed,
behind the dart of its crown, bright yellow.
I couldn't know, he tells me, *what I've seen
without this proof.* If seeing is believing,

belief is photographs. Birds are forever
on the move, so quick and hard to fix
flickering in bushes, while his life, his own,
ticks by uncounted, the world well lost

to this. The camera's set to one thousandth
of a second, an eye ready to open
to its widest for the merest blink of light.
He expounds on critical timing, on apps

and art, and the miracle dawns on me,
wizardry perfected by invention
to see, know and keep this once only, never
to be repeated chance of present beauty.

Fleet Feet

Locked down in a custom-built apartment
in Silicon Valley, he has not touched
anybody for six weeks. Window blinds

filter light, hiding the walls of nearby
buildings and the lack of green, as he works
remotely in front of a desktop screen.

He wakes at dawn, can't sleep on, so goes out
for a run before the day's heat clamps down.
He covers miles to find trees, a small lake,

pauses to look up a bird on his phone:
will add killdeer to his list, green heron.
Gifts everywhere, as he floats his live net

of attention on the speed of his run
to catch every chance of delight. He runs
then stands, quite still, to pay heed and wonder.

Later he'll go to the carry-out and load
gallons of bottled water into the car
for the parched protesters in Oakland.

In the evening – they're under curfew now
with the riots – he notes gifts for the day.
If he writes them down, he remembers,

then remembers more that would otherwise
be lost. Not only birds, wildflowers (he notes
fiddlenecks, redmaids, blue-eyed grass) and three

swallowtail butterflies, but the keen bliss
of iced passion fruit tea, translucent
amber-rose in his glass; a problem solved,

a job completed, and his 'fleet feet'
in their running shoes, the nearest he knows
to being airborne, a gift of flight.

Making Him at Home

We must risk delight – Jack Gilbert

Writing on glass
with her special pen, she letters
wide windows with fragments of poems.

Outside the pane, she attaches
the humming-bird feeder,
and hangs in the bare twiggy bushes beyond

pine cones coated with peanut butter
and primed with seeds,
inviting woodpecker, chickadee, jay;

inviting his watchful stillness
in a reflected brightness that snow
re-directs from midwinter sky

on to his face like wonder.
Formal, gracious, this bend
and re-bound of light will find his own inmost

reflection on what it means to be
here and at home
in himself, in the present

surprise of a day with the sun only just
returning from its outermost
reach and curve.

Day-shine through glass will play on his skin
with shadows of words –
star, perhaps, *cross*, *risk* or *delight*....

So he might raise a hand
to catch in its palm and bring
to his tongue, *heart*, perhaps, *home*,

while there – so close! – a feathered flame
hangs at the feeder,
sipping sweetness.

Joy Ride

I've played the video clip over
and over to find the man, who is tall
and by no means young, huddled and folded
into a sitting crouch on a skateboard,
while the girl, space-child in an orange helmet
and electric-blue jacket, dances around
her captive, checking he's ready for
push-off. Balanced on the fulcrum of hip
and spine, he grips a steepled shin, fields
a rogue foot – then yes, gives her the nod.
I hear the rumble of rollers on tarmac,
her shout of glee. He beams up as he goes,
catching the camera's eye (and mine)
or of someone recording his foolish,
his tender, belittlement: happiness
shines from that look like love's reflection,
with something complicit, pride almost
that this could be done, defiant of
dignity, gravity –
     It's all I have
of the story. Again it starts after
the beginning, ends again before
it's over, losing/recovering/losing
those few seconds. Who knows where
it will lead down the slope –
        gathering speed.

Too Soon to Winter

She knows how it feels, to fold your wings
into their own shadow. There are times
at the edge of her years' winter

when she simply keeps still, her life on hold
for unmeasured minutes more trance
than thought, as if to summon resolve

or recall a dream, as once she would rest
on the fellside and look back over the view
opening, receding, evolving behind her

with every step of the climb, to gaze
almost like flying before the next hard
ascent: the past spread like a broad train,

its manifold scenes lit but diminishing;
the future drawing in, forbidding, steep.
Yet it's too soon, surely, to winter.

She longs to release the butterfly,
a small deckle-edged triangle, darker
than the wall's dark corner where it hides

though the cruel wind has dropped, and scabious
floats intricate mauve-blue orbs on warm air
simmering with a late summer sweetness.

A tickle of panic in her hands' careful
cage, which will open at the open window.
A flicker of flame, its life ignites

for brief moments on her outstretched fingers
before it flits away, veers out of sight,
yet suggests a planing curve which the eye

or the mind follows across the sunlit field
and which a bird takes up over there to sketch
a questing turn, an outward wave of flight.

Gift

Air heavy already with the promise
of heat, so still as to seem a condition
of life, and of her own body sitting
out here on the bench, weight of bones
robed in flesh as resigned and patient
as a morning waiting for nothing
to happen.
         Nothing happening.
                   Until –
could that be a bird in the old lilac
whose crabbed branches invite
fellow-feeling against gravity's ache
over the years? Flicker of leaf, then
a twitch of the light too brief to catch:
a blue tit appears, just appears
on the wall, beak-sipping at the bowl,
hopping right in now, breast-dipping
the shallow water, wings fluttering
in a frenzied wallow of washing.

Everything attends – sultry air, the tree
spellbound – to this one quickness, and she
in her weary pause, reluctant to move
before the day's business starts, borrows
lightness, as water flies from a flurry
of feathers and she sips her morning tea.

Lift-off

You could say he is old now, tacking up
this slope like a sail boat in a head wind,
though the day is serene and cloudless.
Not striding out as once he would have done,
bounding along a summit ridge. How many
mountains, wildernesses, what winds, leagues, heights,
his heart, lungs, bones remember – here in the park,
watching those lads diving for a Frisbee,
that child turning cartwheels, plaits brushing the grass.
Warm sun has drawn out these Sunday crowds
like a festival. How the young delight
in bodies unfreighted with history,
such thoughtless ease. Regretting not a step
of his own, though each one must be careful now.
Under naked trees the girls' bare arms.
Sap is rising, unseen. The hot air balloon
takes leave of the ground at this moment,
wondrously blue and huge like some giant pod
released from the ocean floor, slow-floating
upwards as if air were watery fathoms.
Triangular pennants flutter from guy ropes.
Some kind of effigy dangles there, too,
swinging pale articulate bones. Is it life-size,
larger? Hitching a lift – he can feel it –
his spirit gains height as he watches
that mesmeric drift, higher, smaller.
That potent blue, deeper in tone than the sky's:
blue on blue filling his gaze (expanding
in his head that space opened by how many
distances scanned) so that the trees' bare crowns,
when he looks down, seem to glow green,
rose-gold, as if already flushed with spring.

Before I Can Fly

I am learning to walk in the small hours
with Marianne, tonight's nurse, who tells me
while everyone's sleeping how she attended
the birth of her daughter's twin girls, and I,
with my wealth of sons and grandsons, think
what fortune to be mothered by this wise
woman, an old soul surely in this distaff
line of care and lore reaching through time.
She's checked my vital signs on the machine,
but talks now of the body's ley lines
as she wrings out a cold flannel to fold
round my throat, and the sickness recedes.
She's just behind me on my zimmer trip
to the bathroom. A light touch to my tail
reinforces her words, *Tuck it in, straighten,*
and sends their message the length of my spine
to my neck, lifting my chin, and my view
above and beyond my dithering feet
opens: a corridor lit at intervals
above closed doors. *You have been walking
all your life, you know how.*
                                    Beyond the bend,
beyond the passage of wintering months,
I look down the lane through sycamores, ash
coming into leaf, to the gate on to
the path through Smardale where wood cranesbill
are beginning already to flood the banks
with their rare mauve-blue, among low drifts
of stitchwort, white stars.
                         I'm almost flying.

The Blue Mountain

for S J Litherland

Every card this year covered in flowers
and Eddy arrived with a red and white armful
of daisies, roses, lilies, carnations
so abundant we were at a loss
for a huge enough vase. Is it to console
or sweeten my years, or just a May birthday?
Only you, my companion of hey days and high
passions, of gales and floods and eruptions
of Moet left too long in the freezer,
only you have sent me a mountain.
On its summit, Klee balances its green
reflection at an interface of elements:
an act of aerial circus, peak to sharp
peak, like a kiss at the vanishing point
of past into future, and a view opens
on to a wave of hills, such memories.
How you stepped once, laureate of snow,
up to your thighs in a drift on Dove Crag.
How we'd rave, spreadeagled on heather –
'It's happening!' – as the wild exertion and air
oxygenated our vision so that colours
pulsed and glowed in moor grass, rocks, shadows,
prismatic at the edges of clouds.
So many days, lemon and peacock,
terracotta, earth-dark, of our long friendship
dance in Klee's levity, not of petals
but flags and squares, radiant geometry,
the way we saw the world then, transfigured.

Snow Shadows

Wary always of the worst, seeing the depths
of cloud, its load of bruise, he said it would snow,
while I defied his better judgement,
determined to find one delicate last

strand of sunlight. Who were we to fear snow?
Ice pollen at first, opening parachute
petals to float then swirl like lost spirits
in a world like a snowstorm globe,

where I walked under a glass enchantment,
grinning up at him as I licked crystals
from my lips. That time, he said, plucking it
from my mind, we were covered in minutes.

He meant how intrepid we were back then,
how crazy, on the spine of Place Fell, head on
into the full tilt of the blizzard,
quilted, blinded until we turned our backs

against the storm's drive to look down snow tunnels
forged like shadows by our own bodies through
the spinning light. That time – and here we are
again, forever on the mountain, surprised

to be here still, white with the shaken years.

Tresure

She will tresure my letter forever,
Bethany begins, and four pages follow
with spaces for butterflies. Never before
has she received a real letter.

In mine, I taught her PS for thoughts after the end,
and dream now of sharing a love of brackets
(words in the wings) and commas,
punctuation's breath (the spirit's symbol).

She is sorry, she says, for not adding colour
to her drawings. But she's copied butterflies
with such care that colour flashes subliminally
from tortoiseshell shadows, veined wings;

it breaks through ink and white paper, sped
by those flicked tails on her gs and ys;
through vagaries of spelling and the mail.
PS I will write allot more letters in future.

I can believe in treasure, the quark, genes,
a mirror in the heart, as her pencil attends
to the Comma's groovy wings which, she notes,
don't look pretty at all on the outside

but when they open its brethtaking.

Beyond Me

I've lived long enough
to let the future go,
disclaim its untold stories,

consigning hope to the unknown.
My sons, too, will see their children
weathering heartbreak,

holding the generations in their arms.
The birch tree, too, has weathered storms,
shedding twigs like grief,

swinging its curtains of leaves
in a summer wind, to live on
for a while – as I could hope – beyond me.

Today my first great-grandchild
sleeps glowing in my lap,
skin of pale silk, eyelids flickering:

I can see she is dreaming.

Moss

This is the mission of moss,
the plushing of roots and stones,
small clutches of bones.

This is the cunning of moss,
to hush a creaking glade,
furring the edges of shadows.

This is the stealth of moss, to muffle
a footfall, disguise a pitfall,
its green enfathoming smother.

This is the habit of moss,
the secret undoing of walls.
Consider the patience of moss,

to make quiet the grief
that falls from your heart
like a blue jay's feather.

This is the scent of moss, cool
and forgetful of not quite nothing.
Its taste is bittersweet knowledge.

Granted the mist rising off the lake
to meet the fells' understanding
of cloud, and the seep of time

in a moist wood, moss charms
the path we lost, reclaims the trod,
deploys its spores.

Night Vision

I shall walk away from myself,

shoulder my rucksack of night,
take leave of me standing here

watching my quick stride, straight back,
as if seeing by starlight.

I shall be free of my years,
left behind to remember –

as my eyes follow my own
silhouette receding, black

at the crest of the long road
and never once looking back –

how young I was, the bright sea.

Notes

Page 30 'Swale Time'
split jiffy: Gilbert Newton Lewis (1875–1946) proposed a unit of time called a jiffy, which was equal to the time it takes for light to travel one centimetre in a vacuum (approximately 33.3564 picoseconds).
world line: 'In physics, the world line of an object (approximated as a point in space, e.g. a particle or observer) is the sequence of spacetime events corresponding to the history of the object. A world line is a time-like curve in spacetime. Each point of a world line is an event that can be labelled with the time and spatial position of the object at that time.' Wikipedia

Page 33 'Our Brocken Spectres'
The Order of Time, Carlo Rovelli, 2018

Page 59 'Silversmith Raising a Vase': after a short film, *In the Studio:* Hiroshi Suzuki, 2008, Museum of Art and Design. Definitions from the Shorter Oxford English Dictionary

www.ingramcontent.com/pod-product-compliance
Lightning Source LLC
Chambersburg PA
CBHW042116100526
44587CB00025B/4082